Furthermore

Furthermore

Poems by

Jane Blanchard

© 2025 Jane Blanchard. All rights reserved.
This material may not be reproduced in any form, published,
reprinted, recorded, performed, broadcast,
rewritten, or redistributed without
the explicit permission of Jane Blanchard.
All such actions are strictly prohibited by law.

Cover design by Shay Culligan
Cover art by John Henry Dearle, section of *Seaweed,* 1901

ISBN: 978-1-63980-710-9

Kelsay Books
502 South 1040 East, A-119
American Fork, Utah 84003
Kelsaybooks.com

To Jimmy

Acknowledgments

Poems in this collection have first been published as follows:

Aethlon: "Tiger Woods"
Alabama Literary Review: "Imperative" – "To Carolyn"
Allegro Poetry Magazine: "Of Sheep and Goats"
Arion: "Sisyphus"
Artemis: "The Fish"
The Asses of Parnassus: "The Deal at the Dump" – "Finis" – "Nonce" – "Tit for Tat" – "To Each Her Own" – "Transposition"
Assisi: "Admission"
Autumn Sky Poetry Daily: "Seen and Unseen"
Blue Unicorn: "Caveats" – "Marsh View" – "Modus Operandi" – "Never-Never Land"
Calamaro: "Late December"
Concho River Review: "Pathology"
The Dead Mule School of Southern Literature: "Remembered"
Dear Leader Tales: "Florence"
Dorothy Parker's Ashes: "BED BATH & BEYOND"
The Enigmatist: "Fancy"
First Things: "Lullaby"
The French Literary Review: "Après En Plein Air" – "*Argenteuil Basin with a Single Sailboat*"
Intégrité: "Listen . . ." – "Shepherd . . ."
Light: "Isle Style"
Lighten Up Online: "Almost Advent" – "Care to Share" – "Cohabitation" – "Fault!" – "Folie à Deux" – "Me – Me – Me – Me" – "Mirror, Mirror . . ." – "Oh?"
The Lyric: "Palimpsest" – "To Whom It May Concern"
Orbis: "Mid-Winter" – "Seclusion"
The Orchards Poetry Journal: "Upon the Death of V. S. Naipaul"
Peacock Journal: "Optics"

The Penwood Review: "Hereafter" – "Symbiosis"
The Poeming Pigeon: "Alpha Down Under"
Quatrain.Fish: "Aversion" – "Directive"
The Reach of Song: "Good Doggie"
The Seventh Quarry: "Contorted Filbert" – "Maelstrom"
Ship of Fools: "After Irma" – "Evil" – "Wedding"
Silkworm: "All Hallows' Eve"
Snakeskin: "Limbo" – "Son of Adam" – "Synaesthesia"
Sparks of Calliope: "In Residence"
Third Wednesday: "Unchosen"
Time of Singing: "December" – "Terra Infirma"
U.S.1 Worksheets: "Meal Deal"
Valley Voices: "Between Rounds"
Website of the Bay Area Poets Coalition: "Self-Editing"
Website of the Robert Frost Foundation: "Near the End of Ocean Boulevard"
Website of the Society of Classical Poets: "The Book of Kells" – "Those Days and These"
WestWard Quarterly: "Association"

Poems in this collection have been republished as follows:

Aethlon: "Tiger Woods"
Autumn Sky Poetry Daily: "Seen and Unseen"
Brought to Sight & Swept Away: "Late December"
Extreme Formal Poems: "Mirror, Mirror . . ." – "Symbiosis"
Extreme Sonnets: "All Hallows' Eve"
Nothing Divine Dies: "Near the End of Ocean Boulevard"
The Shepherd's Voice: "Listen . . ." – "Lullaby" – "Shepherd . . ."
The Society of Classical Poets Journal: "The Book of Kells" – "Those Days and These"
Time of Singing: "Limbo"
WestWard Quarterly: "Synaesthesia"

The epigraph of this collection comes from *The Complete Notebooks of Henry James,* edited by Leon Edel and Lyall H. Powers (New York: Oxford UP, 1987), 15.

The epigraph of "Hereafter" comes from the King James Version of the Bible.

Contents

Seen and Unseen	17
Seclusion	18
Isle Style	19
Optics	20
After Irma	21
Association	22
Transposition	23
Mid-Winter	24
Terra Infirma	25
Alpha Down Under	26
In Residence	27
Care to Share	28
Tiger Woods	29
Between Rounds	30
Self-Editing	31
BED BATH & BEYOND	32
Fancy	33
The Book of Kells	34
Me – Me – Me – Me	35
Contorted Filbert	36
Mirror, Mirror . . .	37
Synaesthesia	38
Symbiosis	39
Limbo	40
Après En Plein Air	41
Directive	42
Cohabitation	43
The Deal at the Dump	44
Almost Advent	45
Pathology	46
Son of Adam	47
Sisyphus	48

Palimpsest	49
Admission	50
Meal Deal	51
Caveats	52
Of Sheep and Goats	53
To Whom It May Concern	54
All Hallows' Eve	55
Finis	56
The Fish	57
To Each Her Own	58
Never-Never Land	59
Modus Operandi	60
Near the End of Ocean Boulevard	61
Fault!	62
Wedding	63
Folie à Deux	64
Shepherd . . .	65
Tit for Tat	66
Those Days and These	67
Evil	68
Listen . . .	69
Remembered	70
Good Doggie	71
December	72
Lullaby	73
To Carolyn	74
Hereafter	75
Maelstrom	76
Upon the Death of V. S. Naipaul	77
Marsh View	78
Aversion	79
Unchosen	80

Oh?	81
Imperative	82
Florence	83
Argenteuil Basin with a Single Sailboat	84
Nonce	85
Late December	86

"The *whole* of anything is never told..."

—Henry James

Seen and Unseen

Saint Simon's Island

Wind from the east drives cloud by cloud toward shore—
enormous cotton balls appear to swipe
the too-blue summer sky—their shadows turn
the ocean from dull gray to duller tan.

The tide continues getting higher while
wind from the east drives cloud by cloud toward shore—
the sandbar is submerged—pelicans
routinely glide, then dive-bomb schools of fish.

Swimmers return to help sunbathers move
all chairs and towels out of danger as
wind from the east drives cloud by cloud toward shore—
remaining beverages are soon consumed.

Beyond the seawall stand palmettos, fronds
waving—above them flies a dragon, tail
wiggling, string held by someone not in view—
wind from the east drives cloud by cloud toward shore.

Seclusion

One benefit of living on the coast
is no one knows us here. A few recall
our faces, fewer still our name, but most
just nod or smile or wave in passing. All
we want to do is be polite, not share
more information than is necessary.
Occasionally an extrovert will dare
to get a bit familiar; we are wary
of such and often let an opportune
distraction obviate response. Content
together, we are by and large immune
to any pressure meant to change our bent.
While others seem to socialize with ease,
we go about our business as we please.

Isle Style

Our wardrobes have
Somewhat decayed.

Your pants and shirts
Are rather frayed.

My skirts and tops
Look retrograde.

Your sweaters all
Resemble suede.

My only coat
Is long past trade.

Your belts and ties
Appear ill-made.

My handbag wins
No accolade.

Most shoes and hats
Could use first aid.

At least our love
Has yet to fade.

Optics

Half-time you take a break and go outside,
soon call me to the balcony to gaze
beyond the sunken sandbar—to the left
of all the buoys which direct the boats
and ships and freighters from the river to
the ocean. Could it be a capsized raft
or other vessel? Are those bobbing blobs
real people in the water fore and aft?
Binoculars prove not to be much help
since neither set of eyes works well enough
these days. I still point out the obvious:
no one is flailing. That much I can tell.
But you say nothing and keep looking, so
I recommend you call the Coast Guard or
go back to watching football. You agree
ten minutes later—to the latter—and
game-over (touchdown!) there is nothing there.

After Irma

A major hurricane has hit
    the beach resort again—
It is not difficult to see
    where too much tide has been.

Landscapers pull the old shrubs out
    and put the new ones in—
Perhaps the latter can survive
    a year or two or ten.

Association

The swath of paint now on the ceiling of
the living room is wider/longer than
the one before. Rain entering above
the valence during Irma stretched the span
a lot. Our favorite handy fellow did
his best—each time—to fix the damage by
much scraping, spackling, smoothing—on a bid
to cover natural intrusion. Dry
will get all wet again if those folks who
reside upstairs decline to caulk as asked.
Throughout the winter they are welcome to
ignore the simple maintenance just tasked,
but once the summer comes we do expect
the Golden Rule to go into effect.

Transposition

Years after we were married I
suggested we should simplify:

"Let us forget Saint Valentine
since I am yours and you are mine."

You certainly did not take long
to deem my notion far from wrong:

"That is indeed the thing to do
because we both are tired and true."

Mid-Winter

The fog at noon, as thick as soup, means horns
are sounding in the rivers heading out
to sea. Boats, buoys, other islands have
all vanished seemingly. Faint images
of people on the beach appear, their dogs
more often heard than seen. Low tide does not
reveal the sandbar surely just off-shore.
Around the empty swimming pool are furled
umbrellas. Motionless palmettos stand
nearby. Inside the trendy restaurant
two bowls of steaming seafood bisque are splashed
with sherry, served with salads and warm bread.
A couple sit, say grace, and eat their fill
four days before their Lenten fast begins.

Terra Infirma

Each ghostly crab digs one small hole
    In sand where it can hide
From dangers which too often come
    With rising sun or tide.

At times the need to catch a meal
    Will cause it to emerge
And risk becoming prey to some
    Much larger creature's urge.

Alpha Down Under

> *According to* The Wall Street Journal,
> *Australian miners and ranchers are*
> *confronting a powerful avian enemy.*

The wedge-tailed eagle has the right
To take out any drone in flight.

With size and weight both factored in,
This angry bird is bound to win.

A drone up early in the day
May not be seen as foe or prey.

But no maneuver or disguise
Can guarantee all-friendly skies.

Those drones which undergo attack
Lack any means of fighting back.

Should one be damaged, wrecked, or lost,
Its operator bears the cost.

There really is no fail-safe scheme
To foil the Aussie bird supreme.

In Residence

A challenge of dividing time between
two homes arises in the middle of
the night. One wakes up questioning the scene
of somnolence. Is there a fan above
the bed? How heavy are the covers on
the body? Answers indicate the floor
plan one must walk to reach the nearest john
while not relying on night vision more
than absolutely necessary. (Eyes
once open rarely want to close again
for hours.) With luck, one's better half just sighs,
turns over, goes right back to sleep. A win
comes when one's self succumbs to slumber and
some sprightly man begins to sprinkle sand.

Care to Share

*responding to Facebook's bold
campaign against revenge porn*

If you have ever dared to strike a pose
Without the proper minimum of clothes
And let a lover take a snap or two,
Then broken up, well, here is what to do:
Just send all pictures of your body nude
To Zuckerberg, the "Trust me" Facebook dude,
So he can save each image as a hash
And add them to his very private stash.

Tiger Woods

"Daddy made some mistakes."
—*as quoted in* TIME *Magazine*

I offer an apology
To you, my daughter and my son:
I am as sorry as can be.

I should have gone for courtesy
In games I either lost or won.
I offer an apology.

I should have shown fidelity
And not run after every "hon."
I am as sorry as can be.

I should have dosed—dozed—privately.
(That DUI cost me a ton.)
I offer an apology.

I should have gotten a degree
In how to spin what may be spun.
I am as sorry as can be.

Not all of life is me, me, me.
I need another mulligan.
I offer an apology.
I am as sorry as can be.

Between Rounds

Year after year the very best in golf
head to Augusta. Fans come, too, and those
who live and work here either take time off
to travel or adopt a Masters' pose.
One local woman hosts a party for
alumni of our alma mater. I
attended with my husband once. The hors
d'oeuvres were delicious, drinks well worth a try.
Invitees wandered through the house into
the garden, where the talk had lots of fizz.
One liquored man when asked "What do you do?"
replied: "I fly for Delta—soon to Rome."
My husband looked my way as I looked his;
we both were more than glad to stay at home.

Self-Editing

My wife says that now that I'm older
My speech should be meeker, not bolder.
She wants me to curb
Each noun and each verb.
"Gosh darn it," I've told her and told her.

BED BATH & BEYOND

Needing a break from house and husband, I
go shopping on a Sunday morning by
myself. I reach my destination in
about five minutes, then take maybe ten
to find the items on my list—a set
of towels and two lampshades. Next I get
in line to make my purchases. There is
one station open, its cashier a whiz
at chatting people up while taking care
of business. Waiting for my turn, I stare
as some determined man buys toiletries
with coupon after coupon. To appease
me, his poor wife confides before they go,
"I cannot take him anywhere, you know."

Fancy

If I prefer familiar spaces,
Why should I go to different places?

Because I might find something new
That I could take a liking to.

A sight, a smell, a taste, a sound—
Who knows what image would astound

As well as prompt a poem when
I finally got home again.

The Book of Kells

The intricacies of script and figure are
amazing. Kudos to the faithful who
made contributions large or small. By far
this volume is the greatest ever to
present illuminated gospel. Ink
was carefully applied to skins of calves
bred for this very purpose. Just to think
of such devotion—nothing done by halves—
puts me to shame. As one who tries to craft
a poem now and then for reasons not
exclusively religious, I know—draft
by draft—when I am falling short. No jot
of mine will ever match the artistry
of monks renowned for anonymity.

Me – Me – Me – Me

to Emily

I'll tell you who I am – my dear –
I'm Somebody – for sure!
You – Nobody – from what I hear –
Are utterly obscure.

On Facebook – Twitter – Instagram –
My followers are many!
I like the Bog – in which I am –
As swell a Frog as any.

Contorted Filbert

at Augusta [State] University

Of all the trees and shrubs and flowers on
this campus, you alone are tagged. A strip
of plastic states your name—perhaps so that
grounds maintenance will not mistake you for
something to be removed. Come summer, leaves
will hide your twisted frame; mid-winter, there
exists no panoply of greenery
for gray arthritic branches not yet dead.

Mirror, Mirror . . .

Mirror, Mirror, on the wall,
Do you have to show me all
Failures of myself to meet
Former standards of conceit?

You were purchased way back when:
I was so much younger then,
Thinner and more beautiful;
Wrinkles seemed impossible.

Could you please enhance the view
I am often subject to
As I have to make a pass
Down the hall and by your glass?

If you cannot humor me
And appease my vanity,
I shall need to strategize:
Maybe I should close both eyes.

Synaesthesia

Two Magnolia Blossoms in a Glass Vase
by Martin Johnson Heade, c. 1890

The images appear so real—
The challenge is to look, not touch.
How do those luscious petals feel?
The images appear so real!
Slick leaves, soft velvet, too, appeal
To all who gaze amazed at such.
The images appear so real—
The challenge is to look, not touch!

Symbiosis

All summer long the roses thrive,
Those thorny plantings with the drive
To stretch toward heaven day by day,
While grapevines slowly wind their way
As far as rugged roots contrive.

If heat and moisture should connive,
The vineyard's owner will derive
A warning from the blooms' display
      All summer long.

Before the mildew can deprive
The lot of means to stay alive,
Vine-tenders must apply a spray
So fruits as well as flowers may
Enhance their chances to survive
      All summer long.

Limbo

You know it needs to end.
The question then is when,
For why should you extend
Again and yet again?

More will not let you mend,
Nor make a loss a win.
The doctor is no friend
If treatment does you in.

Après En Plein Air

*upon the microscopic inspection
of Vincent van Gogh's* Olive Trees
at the Nelson-Atkins Museum of Art

There it has been since 1889—
a grasshopper—or what remains of one—
buried in swirls of paint. The lush design
of olive trees comes from a series done
despite confinement in the south of France.
This version is superb—the foliage green
and full—the trunks, though brown and gnarled, still dance,
their shadows mottled blue, the ground between
a mix of neutral tones—red flowers pop
up on the left—the sky above/behind
looks indigo. Such beauty could not stop
the fluctuations of a troubled mind,
whose work an expert tries to analyze
only to find an insect post-demise.

Directive

When working on my epitaph
    Soon after I have died,
Keep effort to a minimum
    And chisel out, "She tried."

Cohabitation

There lives a hound in my backyard.
Ignoring it is very hard.
It barks a lot each blessèd day.
It hears a car and starts to bay.
It leaps to greet the neighbor's dogs.
It runs at squirrels and jumps on frogs.
It scares the birds from any tree.
It ruins lawn and shrubbery.
It digs up pipes laid underground.
It chews on everything around.
Why does my son plead this hound's case?
He cannot pay for their own place.

The Deal at the Dump

How totally appropriate
As end of year approaches:
The White House is infested with
Ants, mice, and—yes!—cockroaches.

This news is likely genuine
According to work orders:
Not even Trump can turn such pests
From squatters into boarders.

Almost Advent

So sorry to take you to task,
But there is something I must ask:

When will you ever eat the last
Brach*s peppermint from Christmas past?

Pathology

The man had made his living in a lab.
Once he retired, his health took up his time—
at home, then not. His wife, the queen of gab,
confided he had choked—despite the prime
expense of private care, a pill had done
him in. "How horrible," I sympathized,
delivering fresh bread. She, never one
for warmth, endured my hug and exercised
remarkable composure. I was less
successful—tears impeded any deft
departure. Hearing science would assess
the husband who had left her so bereft,
I thought but dared not ask, "An autopsy?"
She answered anyway, "For family."

Son of Adam

Reconcile yourself to toil
As you stand on stubborn soil.

Try to make the ground relax
With a spade or hoe or axe.

Use whatever implement
To the maximum extent.

Always do your very best
Till you, too, are laid to rest.

Sisyphus

I roll the boulder up the hill.
The boulder rolls back down again.
There is to be no standing still.

My efforts take no thought or skill;
The next is what the last has been:
I roll the boulder up the hill.

Repeatedly, I find no thrill
In this relentless discipline.
There is to be no standing still.

Time after time, the selfsame drill
Gets old and even older when
I roll the boulder up the hill.

The chance of any change is nil.
Since I am doomed, to my chagrin,
There is to be no standing still.

According to some greater will,
The boulder rolls its rolls, and then
I roll the boulder up the hill.
There is to be no standing still.

Palimpsest

Deep lies a trace
of how this race
lived prior to the fall.

Above it sin
has brush-stroked in
the doom of death for all.

Yet higher still
appears God's will
for those who heed His call.

Admission

As if compelled by love to come,
A daughter shows up at my door.
My shock must be recovered from.
As if compelled by love to come
Inside, she does, and we talk some.
I cannot help but long for more,
As if compelled by love to come:
A daughter shows up at my door.

Meal Deal

My son, though very busy, must
    Enjoy my company;
Invited to an evening out,
    He often will agree.

The usual location is
    The Titleholders bar;
From work or home, for both of us,
    The drive is not too far.

A smiling server offers me
    My favorite Chardonnay;
My son prefers to order beer,
    Some on-tap IPA.

He has a Dusty Bunny or
    Goes for a Wicked Weed;
We drink until our food arrives
    And supper can proceed.

We chat about his job in sales,
    My life with poetry;
I gladly grab the tab for such
    Conviviality.

Caveats

I get along with poetry,
that is, when it enhances me
and records of submission prove
my efforts move or even groove.

Yet poets, on the other hand,
can be impossible to stand,
especially when they brag about
where they are in and I am out.

Of Sheep and Goats

There seems to be some suction going on—
among bagpipers nonetheless. Band-size
affects the odds of winning any prize
at competition. In a blow-a-thon
bigger is better, not just louder, since
impressive music can be played. A score
of kilts thus outperforms a dozen. Sore
about the loss, the twelve posthaste convince
another twelve to join their ranks. Next time
a band of thirty is the champion—
and so it goes. If tuning may be done,
more pipes (plus drums) will stay the paradigm.
The effort to turn rivals into mates
increases faith that victory awaits.

To Whom It May Concern

Our friendship lasted many years
Of sharing either laughs or tears.

I noticed, though, I did too much,
Compared to you, to stay in touch.

Eventually, I took a break—
Your non-response was no mistake.

The thought of you, from that time on,
Has often made me woebegone.

All Hallows' Eve

Ten days ago the mums appeared to be
as fresh as daisies. Seven ninety-nine
was all they cost—an opportunity
to bring some autumn cheer to me and mine.

Unsheathed and trimmed, the sturdy stalks stood well
haphazardly arranged, the vase antique,
the water fortified. I could not tell
where gold turned red on blossoms at their peak.

Such beauty does not last, of course. Decline
occurs. Now, outer petals droop, most leaves
are curled, the once-clear glass of etched design
displays the dirtiness decay achieves.

So cycles go. Nature will have its way.
Tomorrow I may toss the whole bouquet.

Finis

The end of life comes for us all,
Perhaps too soon, perhaps too late;
Death has its own grim protocol
Re: any expiration date.

The Fish

Alaska, late July

One woman loved her greatest catch
    Despite the fact he died;
His coffin loaded in her truck,
    She took him for a ride.

From town to town and isle to isle
    She drove day after day;
Short stops for gas and food and ice
    Did not cause much delay.

Most folks she met along the route
    Thought her more sad than odd;
One busy-body called police:
    "She's got a corpse, by God!"

At least the woman was not charged
    With any sort of crime;
Was she so wrong to keep her catch
    A little past his time?

To Each Her Own

An earnest widow wants to marry—
I wonder, "How unnecessary!"

She yearns for what she had down pat—
I ponder, "Wow! Been there, done that!"

Never-Never Land

I have attended many conferences,
workshops, retreats, et cetera. West Chester
does not appear on my c.v. Po-biz
gets complicated once some power-wrester
becomes involved. I almost traveled to
the Pennsylvania venue more than once,
but campus politics showed who was who
repeatedly, and I despise such stunts.
The irony is that I write in form,
i.e., the rhyming, metered work disdained
too often since free verse became the norm
for sharing any notion unrestrained.
In truth, though, there is probably no place
where poets like myself meet face to face.

Modus Operandi

That critic targets anyone
    He holds in disregard—
He slings his temper stone by stone
    And hopes the hits are hard.

Sometimes he even aims at those
    Whose style is anodyne—
He must not know more flies are caught
    With sweetness than with brine.

Near the End of Ocean Boulevard

The county's latest bulwark has begun
to fail already—maybe only weeks
since normal traffic was allowed back on
this busy stretch of road. Saltwater seeps,
then undermines concrete too easily.
No engineer has figured out a way
to stop erosion here. Predictably
tides entering and leaving every day
will do their damage. Nature takes care of
its own—the egrets, herons, ibises,
wood storks, and clapper rails which perch above
or nest in marsh grass after meals. What is
a human being in this habitat?
A passerby who gets a glance, if that.

Fault!

Officials are on full alert
At Wimbledon's All England Club!
Their special mission? To avert
In any match a major flub

Involving not technique per se
But rather clothing *à la mode*.
The first and foremost rule of play?
Adherence to a white dress code

Which limits even coloured trim,
Prohibits darker underwear.
Woe be to wacky her or him
Whose tacky logo draws a stare!

That rogue offender will be told
To right at once the wrong attire.
Tradition here, however old,
Is never likely to expire.

Wedding

Some twenty chairs are on the beach—
Ten yards beyond the ocean's reach.

Guests soon arrive to meet or greet—
Still smiling each then takes a seat.

The bride and groom themselves appear—
Attendants and a priest draw near.

The service starts, some word is read—
Two rings are given, vows are said.

The couple kisses, turns to walk—
A laughing gull begins to squawk.

We uninvited leave our perch—
Above the rocks behind this church.

As we proceed, we say a prayer—
"God bless the ones just married there."

Folie à Deux

It happens all too often, sad to say:
Some he and she hook up, decide to wed,
Then let a mutual delusion sway
Them from the truth they should believe instead.

No counterargument finds any way
To disabuse the minds of those misled,
Since reason on its own cannot allay
A fallacy conceived in fancy's bed.

Shepherd . . .

Shepherd, lead us in the way
You would have us go each day;
May we follow here or there,
Ever in your loving care.

Shepherd, rouse us with your rod
Should we need a gentle prod;
We are often unaware,
Even of your loving care.

Shepherd, calm us with your staff,
Close at hand on our behalf;
We are ever prone to scare,
Even in your loving care.

Shepherd, keep us in the fold;
Help us do as we are told,
Not to wander off somewhere
Far beyond your loving care.

Tit for Tat

If deeds, then words, destroy trust,
A partnership can turn to dust.

When all is done and all is said,
One might be mad, the other dead.

Those Days and These

"'... Macbeth does murther sleep.'"
—William Shakespeare

If only such a villain were
    Alone in this regard,
The course of human history
    Would prove to be less hard.

Mythology and scripture are
    Replete with deadly deeds
Conducted by those seeking to
    Meet wants as well as needs.

No time, no place, no culture has
    Been spared the ugly strife
In which some individual
    Cuts short another's life.

The crime, however plotted, tends
    To take a double toll:
It kills the victim's body and
    The perpetrator's soul.

Evil

Why must it always be a woman's fault?
Pandora opened (oops!) a jar, and Eve
took and ate (woops!) the fruit, if we believe
such long-related myths. Neither could halt
what happened afterward—the history,
the art, the literature which cast blame on
her then and always. Innocence once gone
is gone for good—the female legacy!
Yet hope remains. The jar was closed before
that could escape. The loss of Eden led
to Bethlehem. No person needs to dread
the future or regret the past. No score
between the sexes matters. Human themes
are inessential to much grander schemes.

Listen . . .

Listen, sheep, both strong and weak,
Listen to your Shepherd speak.

Since He knows and loves you so,
He will guide you as you go.

If you let Him have the lead,
He will meet your every need.

Hoping to increase His flock,
He takes morn- and evening stock.

When you wander from the fold,
He will bring you back to hold.

Should some danger cause alarm,
He will keep you safe from harm.

Lamb newborn or sheep long-grown,
For your life, He gave His own.

Remembered

A little Jimmy said his prayers
With Momma Anne each night;
While kneeling on a single bed,
He leaned toward what was meet and right.

Compared to "Now I Lay Me Down,"
The Creed set up some hurdles;
Those leapt, he finished with "God bless
The birds, the rabbits, the dogs, and the turtles."

Good Doggie

by Enoch Wood Perry, 1864

Do you want another treat?
Look at me, yes, eye to eye.
Beg if you would like to eat.

There you go. You are so sweet!
Yet still hungry? My, oh, my!
Do you want another treat?

How about this bit of meat?
Such is sure to satisfy.
Leap if you would like to eat.

Well done, doggie! That was neat!
Who knew you could go so high?
Do you want another treat?

How about a different feat?
Can you do it? Why not try?
Twirl if you would like to eat.

Out of tricks? Should we repeat?
Soon I have to say goodbye.
Do you want another treat?
Beg if you would like to eat.

December

It is not wrong to feel a little sad
at any time of year—yes, even now.
Since naturally you miss what you once had,
it is not wrong to feel a little sad.
So listen to me: grieve—and let me add,
if asked, I happily will show you how.
It is not wrong to feel a little sad
at any time of year—yes, even now.

Lullaby

Sleep, baby, sleep, at long last born
In Bethlehem as once foretold,
To parents recently forlorn,
To all who yet may be consoled.

Sleep, baby, sleep, and do not cry
When shepherds from the fields appear,
Just after angels in the sky
Have sung that Christ the Lord is near.

Sleep, baby, sleep, you need not stir
Though weary wise men humbly bring
Gold, frankincense, and even myrrh,
Fine gifts for any earthly king.

Sleep, baby, sleep, as ox and ass
Behold the Son of One "I AM";
So age to age will come to pass
Till lion shall lie down with lamb.

To Carolyn

on whose birthday I was born

I learned of your last illness, then your death,
through lawyers. How I hope you had no fears
of leaving. How I pray your final breath
was not a rant against someone with years,
months, days remaining—namely Jane. Our lives
were bound by common parents who misused
us willfully. One daughter yet survives—
mere me, the younger one, who long refused
to bow to power—for better, not for worse,
I hope and pray again—however hard
is left the effort to escape the curse
of any generation. So, on guard
as always, never mind the customary,
I offer this as your obituary.

Hereafter

*"There the wicked cease from troubling;
and there the weary be at rest."*
                              —Job 3:17

I do look forward to the lack
Of any sort of sneak attack
By cormorant or toad or snake
For nothing less than evil's sake.

Without the need to watch my back
I shall let even wits go slack
And learn to take a welcome break
From always staying wide awake.

Maelstrom

You fall into the vortex of
What pulls you far from all above.

You may yet get the chance to go
Back to the site where life seemed slow.

Or you could surface in a space
Where each new day runs some new race.

Or you might die down in the deep
And make your final peace with sleep.

Upon the Death of V. S. Naipaul

He really should have been more kind
And bought his wife a wedding ring.
Did he not know that she would mind

The lack of such? Though he could find
Some prostitute who did not cling,
He really should have been more kind

To one reliably inclined
To do for him most anything.
Did he not know how she would mind

A mistress, who herself would wind
Up lonely after quite a fling?
He really should have been more kind

To either woman left behind
So he could take what life might bring.
Did he not know that each would mind?

Or were these women both resigned
To roles beyond embarrassing?
He really should have been more kind.
Did he not know? Did they not mind?

Marsh View

Ducks do not seek to be admired,
Except by their own kind, of course,
Whose sidelong glances reinforce
The primal need to be desired.

What follows is a feathered show,
Where one plus one is not enough:
A male proves he is up to snuff
By having two females in tow.

Aversion

My rival and I struck a deal
    Without a fuss or fight:
When passing in a public place,
    We both look to the right.

Unchosen

None of my sonnets won a Nemerov
Despite a decade's worth of entries. Why?
Were my rhymes awkward? Was my meter off?
(Of seventy feet, several can go awry.)
Or were my topics too conventional,
My images too few and far between?
Or was my syntax lax, my diction dull,
My deeper meaning difficult to glean?
Who knows? Each SASE brought results:
First-place and finalists—twelve names in all—
A blurb in which some friendly judge exults,
"Outstanding work!" At odds with protocol,
I wished the screener would less often pick
The fourteen-liners of a certain clique.

Oh?

> *"Scotland has more than 400 words and expressions for snow, according to a project to compile a Scots thesaurus."*
> —*BBC News website*

The Scots, so good to know,
Spout many words for snow,
Far more than ever flow
From any Eskimo.

As Glasgow linguists crow
The list may well yet grow,
Let me just say, "Good show!"
Who understands Scots, though?

Imperative

Forget me not when all is done.
Regardless of which side has won,
I certainly shall think of you,
The former near-and-dear ones who
Allowed malevolence its run.

You reckoned me a simpleton,
A woman you could use, then shun;
If only love had led you to
      Forget me not.

Yet even in this garrison,
I hear a distant clarion:
Each one of you may someday rue
The stress and strain you put me through.
Should peace be sought and there be none,
      Forget me not.

Florence

9/11/2018

America faces a serious threat,
So government sources inform.
The danger's as bad as a danger can get
When weather and words become warm.

This hurricane could be the worst ever yet
Since nature departs from the norm.
"It's tremendously big and tremendously wet,"
The President says of the storm.

Argenteuil Basin with a Single Sailboat

by Claude Monet, 1874

What a dazzling autumn day
for a young Monsieur Monet
to set out upon the Seine
and to use a brush again.

From a roving studio
he sees sky and water flow
as a canvas gets reflective
of his own unique perspective.

Trees arrayed in red and gold
make the scene so manifold
that there is no longing for
what lies on the distant shore.

Recreation fills the hours
of a man with special powers
to preserve a sparkling view
of much more than white and blue.

Nonce

Weather here—
Weather there—
Weather happens everywhere.

June to May—
Night to day—
Such a changing world we share!

High or low—
Fast or slow—
Many figures to compare.

East from west—
Worst from best—
Stormy, cloudy, windy, fair?

South and north—
Back and forth—
Forecasts all too often err.

Cold to hot—
Wet to not—
What is one supposed to wear?

Hard or light—
Strong or slight—
Better offer up a prayer!

Front from back—
Straight from slack—
Circle finally turns square.

Late December

Saint Simon's Island

Although the solstice was a week ago,
the sun still rises slightly later than
it did the day before. I, too, am slow
these winter mornings, yet I keep my plan
of looking toward whatever lies ahead.
By nine I do start walking on the beach
past gulls and grackles, following the tread
of someone faster, endeavoring to reach
the common turning point. The tidal foam
slides over any shells the sand can hold;
I pick none up, reverse my course for home,
increase my pace, now braced against the cold.
Three, no, four jets make silver streaks through clear
blue sky; their contrails form, fade, disappear.

About the Author

A native Virginian, Jane Blanchard lives and writes in Georgia. She has earned degrees in English from Wake Forest and Rutgers universities. Her previous longer collections from Kelsay Books are *Metes and Bounds* (2023), *Sooner or Later* (2022), *Never Enough Already* (2021), *In or Out of Season* (2020), *After Before* (2019), and *Tides & Currents* (2017), following the shorter *Unloosed* (2016).

www.ingramcontent.com/pod-product-compliance
Lightning Source LLC
Chambersburg PA
CBHW071011160426
43193CB00012B/2008